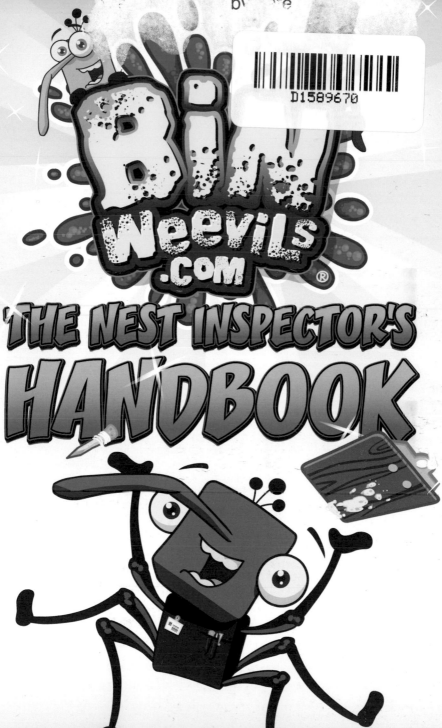

First published 2012 by Macmillan Children's Books
a division of Macmillan Publishers Limited
20 New Wharf Road, London N1 9RR
Basingstoke and Oxford
Associated companies throughout the world
www.panmacmillan.com

ISBN 978-1-4472-0535-7

1 3 5 7 9 8 6 4 2

A CIP catalogue record for this book is available from
the British Library.

Printed and bound in China

CONTENTS

MEET THE NEST INSPECTOR 6

HOW TO SHOW ME YOUR NEST 8

BEST NEST MAGAZINE 10

HOW TO IMPRESS ME 12

SHOP TILL YOU DROP 14

OFF THE WALL 18

FROM TOP TO BOTTOM 20

SNAP UP A SEAT 22

TOP OF THE TABLE 24

SNUG AS A BUG 26

SPECTAC-LOO-LAR 28

WHAT'S COOKIN'? 30

ZING'S ZANY GADGETS 32

ARTY PARTY 34

LIGHT UP YOUR LIFE 36

ARE YOU A FAN? 38

WHAT'S YOUR NEST DÉCOR STYLE? 40

MIRROR MAZES 42

PALACE LUXURY 44

CELEBRITY STYLE 46

THINK TINK 48

FAIRYTALE FANTASY 50

SWEET AS CANDY 52

LET'S PARTY! 54

SPORTS FAN 56

BIN CIRCUS 58

UNDER THE SEA 60

SUPER SAFARI 62

SPACED OUT 64

ENCHANTED FOREST 66

LOOPY LABORATORY 68

HOLIDAY SPIRIT 70

MEDIWEEVIL TIMES 72

PICK YOUR BUDGET 74

COLOUR PLAY 80

TROPHIES 82

SNAP-HAPPY 84

SPECIAL NEST ITEMS 86

CELEB CRIBS 88

SPOT THE DIFFERENCE 90

MUDDLED MESSAGE & PENCIL PUZZLER 92

DID YOU KNOW? 94

GOODBYE 95

ANSWERS 96

MEET THE NEST INSPECTOR

Ah, hello there! No need to knock! Come in, come in!

I wish you a weevily welcome to my Handbook. You've come to the right place for some absolutely fabulous decorating tips, and all the inside info about making your nest look gorgeously grand! Shhh . . . I wouldn't tell this to just anyone, but I can see that you've got a good eye for fine design.

Oh! Did I forget to introduce myself? I'm the one and only Nest Inspector, and BIN-terior design is my passion! Every Bin Weevil wants to get their hands on one of my brilliant trophies – wouldn't you like to know how to get one of your own?

Read on, and I'll tell you how to get your nest into tip-top shape!

The Nest   The Nest Inspector   Inspector

THE NEST INSPECTOR'S FACT FILE

BEST MOMENT
Discovering a trophy-winning nest!

FAVOURITE FOOD
After a long day of nest-inspecting, I like to have a spot of tea and treat myself to a Bin Scone at Figg's Cafe!

FAVOURITE HANGOUT
I love going on holidays, and Mulch Island Beach is the place to be! I always feel most inspired at the beach – a touch of nature is a lovely addition to any nest!

FAVOURITE ELEMENT OF BIN-TERIOR DESIGN
I love a good wallpaper! If you buy just one nest item, make sure it's a fabulous wallpaper. It can transform your whole room in seconds.

FUTURE PLANS
I love to travel and I've seen many spectacular places. I want to create some new travel-themed nest items based on my travels!

7

HOW TO SHOW ME YOUR NEST

Got a dazzling nest? Show it off!

To submit your nest for inspection, you'll need to be a Bin Tycoon member and have a certain nest score. To find out if your nest is ready for inspection yet, click on your Bin Tycoon Camera icon. If your nest is ready, you'll see a special new icon show up above your camera! Snap some pics with pride and send them over to me for a peek, and you might just find a shiny Bin Nest Trophy in your My Stuff Box!

Check out this amazingly awesome award-winning nest!

TOP TIP

You don't have to have lots of Mulch to make an award-winning nest! Just decorate with flair to catch my eye!

Win a brilliant Bin Nest Trophy!

If your nest is really and truly impressive, I'll award you a glittering Bin Nest Trophy in bronze, silver or gold. These trophies are exclusive, and I mean EXCLUSIVE – you'll never see one of these for sale in a shop! Your Bin Buddies will fall over with awe when they spot one of these beauties sitting on your coffee table!

WOW! These fabulous rooms won the GOLDEN Bin Nest Trophy!

Scribbles' nest
NEST SCORE: 1224635

Nest Score → → →

Your nest score changes whenever you redecorate your nest – the better your items, the higher your score. To help your nest score go up even faster, invite lots of guests to your nest! Getting loads of good nest ratings will boost your nest score, and you'll earn some XP, too. Marvellous!

BEST NEST MAGAZINE

NOT ONLY AM I A NEST EXPERT EXTRAORDINAIRE, I ALSO PUBLISH MY VERY OWN MAGAZINE!

Goodness knows where I find the energy – I think it's almost time for another vacation! Mustn't work too hard . . .

Me in Mexico!

Me at the Temple!

Fisherman's Island

Oh, but back to business. Where was I? Right! My magazine.

BEST NEST is its name, and beautiful nests are its flame. No, that's not right . . . its *tame*? No . . . *game*? No . . . *fame*? Fame! Ah, of course! Beautiful nests are its feme.

On each page of my mag, you'll find stunning images of some of the best nests I've seen lately – guaranteed to amaze and inspire. And best of all, they're designed by YOU! Oooh la la!

BEST NEST

HOW TO IMPRESS ME

How do I pick out a top nest? Well, I have a meticulous eye for detail, if I do say so myself! Here are a few of my top tips for creating a nest that will knock my six socks off.

FILL 'EM UP!

Decorate all your rooms as fully as you can! You don't have to pack every nook and cranny, but empty space is not so nice. Make the most of your space, from floor to ceiling!

THEME IT!

Themes are a real treat, so think about having a theme for each room. I've included some glorious ideas for themes later on in this book – check out pages 44–73!

LIGHT IT UP!

You can't see much in the dark, so pop some lights on to make sure your rooms really dazzle. Don't forget to top up your Fuel-o-Meter, too!

COLLECT IT!

I just love a nice arrangement of collectibles. Zing has loads of awesome gadgets for you to choose from!

COLOUR IT!

If you're leaving any of your walls or floors bare, make sure you have a play with the colour sliders in each room to create just the right base shade.

LEVEL UP!

Keep up the hard work and keep levelling up! As you get to higher levels, more extraordinary items will become available to you.

Visit lots of other Bin Weevils' nests and check out BEST NEST magazine for inspiration!

BEST NEST

BEST NEST

13

SHOP TILL YOU DROP!

READY TO START DECORATING?

Let's head over to the Shopping Mall, where you'll find everything your weevily heart desires! It's open 24 hours a day, every single day of the year!

OUTSIDE THE SHOPPING MALL

INSIDE THE SHOPPING MALL

BIN PET SHOP

A nest just isn't a home without a cute little Bin Pet! You can buy a Bin Pet and all the accessories you need at the Bin Pet Shop. How about a stylish Bin Pet Palace for your little friend?

GARDEN SHOP

Make sure your nest is as pretty on the outside as it is on the inside! The Garden Shop has all you need – statues, garden furniture, fancy fences . . . and of course, seeds to grow loads of gorgeous flowers!

PROPERTY SHOP

Running out of room for all that cool stuff you've been buying? Luckily for you, Rigg's construction crew are quick workers! Pop into the Property Shop if you need a new nest room, and Rigg will have you sorted out faster than you can say 'Mulch!'

NEST FLOOR PLANS

TOP TIP

The more rooms you have, the faster your nest score will accumulate because you can earn nest ratings for each and every room!

15

SHOP TILL YOU DROP!

NESTCO

The Mall is my go-to destination whenever I start to feel a bit blue (second only to the beach!) Shopping — even if it's just window-shopping — is always a great pick-me-up! Why not try sketching a room design featuring some of the coolest items you see?

Nestco and Bin Mart are two of my favourite shops! There's nothing you can't find in here — they stock everything from gadgets to furniture and so much more! Plus, they've got some of the wackiest and cleverest shopkeepers around!

BIN MART

Every time you buy an item from the Shopping Mall, you earn XP, which will help you level up more quickly. More expensive items tend to reward you with more XP

I got a chance to interview some of the Bin Weevils who work in th Shopping Mall. Here's what Zing, Fab, Grunt and Flem had to say!

GADGETS & GIZMOS

ZING

ZING SAYS:

Oooh! There's nothing I love more than gadgets! Need a Hologram Projector? A Toy Helicopter? A Lava Lamp? Can I interest you in a cool collectible? It's all about the details, and trust me, I've got all the gizmos you need – from teeny-tiny to extra-colossal.

FLOORS, WALLS & CEILINGS

FAB

FAB SAYS:

Floors, walls, ceilings . . . I don't know which I like best, so I just bounce from one to the next! It's all just so FAB! Brighten up your nest with a splash of colour and a coordinating carpet. Come in and let me spoil you with all the choice you can handle!

KITCHENS & BATHROOMS

GRUNT

GRUNT SAYS:

I don't talk much, but if you want to talk plumbing, there's no one else better for the job. You might think a toilet's just a toilet, but you're wrong! This right here? You're looking at a medal-winning loo!

FURNITURE

FLEM

FLEM SAYS:

I've got all kinds of furniture, from beds and sofas to lights and shelves! You need it, I've got it. *SNIFF* I've even got some hay fever, but I don't think you want that!

17

OFF THE WALL

Walls are a blank canvas waiting to be decorated! Aah . . . just looking at a blank wall really brings out my inner artist. Here are a few of my favourite wall decorations.

MULCH NOTE WALLPAPER

Walls with a View
Fancy opening your curtains to see a spectacular seaside or a dazzling desert?

DESERT VIEW

LAKE VIEW RAINBOW

SURFER BEACH VIEW

Wallpapers

Spice up those drab walls in moments with a wicked wallpaper!

BUBBLY FISH

WORLD MAP

CHOCOLATE BOX

RAINBOW SWEETS

LUCKY CLOVER

Windows

Let a little light shine in with some wonderful windows! Even when it's dark or dreary outside, you can make your nest into your own tiny paradise.

BIN VIEW

SUNSET VIEW

GAM CLOCK

MULCH CLOCK

BIN PET CLOCK

Clocks

It's always the best time of your life with these terrific timepieces!

BONBON CLOCK

FROM TOP TO BOTTOM

Floors aren't just for walking on, you know. Don't settle for boring, deck them out! And don't forget those ceilings – the sky's the limit!

COOL CEILINGS

SEA FLOWER

LITTLE SWEETS

PUFFY PINK

FUNKY FLOORS

ROCK CAFE

GLOSSY GRASS

FANCY FLORAL

20

CASTLE GAM

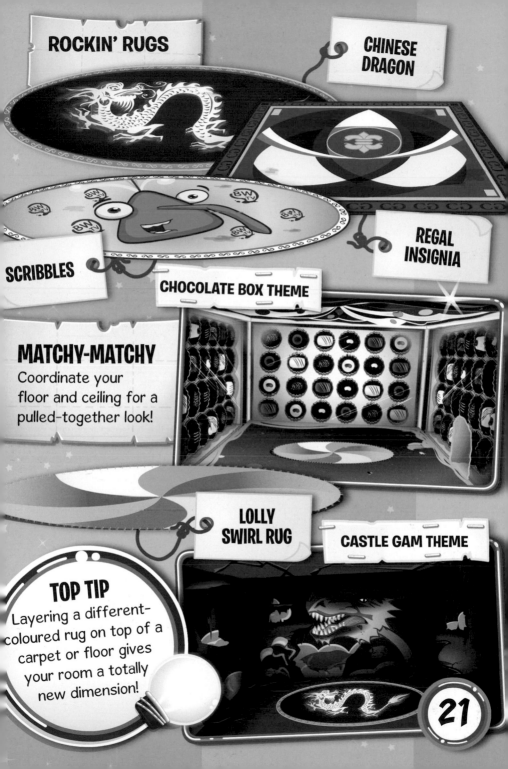

ROCKIN' RUGS

CHINESE DRAGON

REGAL INSIGNIA

SCRIBBLES

CHOCOLATE BOX THEME

MATCHY-MATCHY
Coordinate your floor and ceiling for a pulled-together look!

LOLLY SWIRL RUG

CASTLE GAM THEME

TOP TIP
Layering a different-coloured rug on top of a carpet or floor gives your room a totally new dimension!

21

SNAP UP A SEAT

Your nest is a place to relax and put your weevily feet up, so having somewhere comfy to sit is essential! Here are my top ten picks.

10

HANGING POD CHAIR

9

Chocolate eggs are not just for Easter!

CHOCOLATE EGG CHAIR

MUSHROOM SEAT

8

7

PINK BIRD STOOL

This Mushroom Seat is part of the Tink's Tree Nest Item Collection!

6

Sassy600 designed this chair as part of a competition!

5

HANGING LEAF SEAT

WOODEN THRONE

BURGER THRONE

4

3

LIPS CHAIR

1

ROYAL THRONE

2

SCRIBBLES PILLOW SEAT

ⓘ The Royal Throne is the Bin's most expensive and jewel-encrusted chair! No wonder it's Dosh's favourite!

TOP OF THE TABLE

I bet your nest is just bursting with all that weevily awesome stuff you've been stockpiling. Clott once solved his storage problem by piling up all his items into a giant pyramid. It toppled over and he was stuck under the pile for hours! Aaaargh!

DON'T WORRY, THERE'S A MUCH SMARTER SOLUTION.
Lots of small items can sit on top of other items, so stock up on terrific tables and show-stopping shelves!

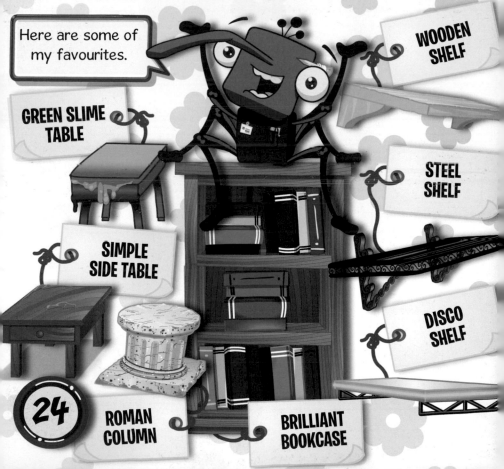

Here are some of my favourites.

WOODEN SHELF

GREEN SLIME TABLE

STEEL SHELF

SIMPLE SIDE TABLE

DISCO SHELF

ROMAN COLUMN

BRILLIANT BOOKCASE

BOX SHELVES RULE!
Switch 'em, stack 'em, mix 'em up! Flem says there are 101 different ways to use these in a nest room . . . I've counted 88 so far!

BOX SHELF

GLASS SHELF

TOP TIP
If you've got an eye-catching wallpaper and you don't want to block it from view, a glass shelf is a perfect pick!

SNUG AS A BUG

After a busy day in the Bin, you'll want to snuggle down in one of these soft and stylish beds. It's so hard to choose — I've got a different bed for every day of the week!

CHOCO CAKE BED

ROCKET SHIP BED

REGAL BED

PIRATE SHIP BED

WOODEN ARC BED

HEART BED

PINK PRINCESS BED

SCRIBBLES BED

CLOTT BED

TINK BED

BUNTY BED

EASTER BASKET BED

FOOTBALL BED

GOLD CROWN BED

TOP TIP

Want to gaze up at some of your favourite trophies? Why not put a shelf full of your achievements right above your bed? Nothing like a sense of accomplishment to get you out of bed in the morning!

27

SPECTAC-LOO-LAR

I simply adore my bubble baths, so my bathroom is one of the most important rooms in my nest. And don't ever say that toilets don't matter – at least, not in front of Grunt!

SQUARE JACUZZI

BATHROOM COMBINATIONS

BATHROOM SINK

MIRRORS

TOWEL RACK

HAUNTED TOILET

SLIMY TOILET

BLING TOILET

Make yourself comfortable!

CLASSIC SHOWER

SIMPLE BATHTUB

ROLL-TOP BATHTUB

TOP TIP

Choose a tiled wall to keep the damp at bay. There are loads of different colours to choose from!

RAINBOW WALL TILES

29

WHAT'S COOKIN'?

If you want to learn to cook as well as Tum or Figg, you're going to need a fully equipped kitchen. And even if you can't cook . . . well, you still need somewhere to put your microwave and coffee machine!

Check out these two kitchen rooms! They're so hot they're on fire!

RETRO STYLE

CLASSICALLY COOL

Flamin' awesome wallpapers!

DISHWASHER

COOKER

POPCORN MACHINE

30

CHOCOLATE MAKER

COFFEE MACHINE

RETRO FRIDGE

FIRE EXTINGUISHER

ROUND MICROWAVE

SILVER KETTLE

FLOWERY TOASTER

TEAPOT & TEACUP

HANGING POT RACK

TOP TIP

Some of the level trophies look a lot like tasty food! There's no better place to show these off than on top of your kitchen cupboards. Don't let your buddies eat them, though!

31

ZING'S ZANY GADGETS

Zing's got a lot of cool gadgets, but watch your step! Some of these gadgets have minds of their own! Check out some of Zing's top-selling items.

MAGIC ICE CUBE

GADGET TABLE

TRANSFORMING TABLE

ZANY LIGHTS

TOP TIP
Try clicking on your gadgets to bring them to life!

UPSIDE-DOWN CHAIR

GADGET-MAKER

X-RAY MACHINE

ROBOT BIN PET

WEEVILY VACUUM

CAMERA ROBOT

Zing is the Bin's gadget expert, and she's even tried her hand at making some herself! Wow!

33

ARTY PARTY

So you've put up some ultra-cool wallpaper, but your wall just doesn't seem complete? You need the perfect wall art to complement it! How about a neon sign, a poster, or even a chalkboard? Possibilities, my friends – explore them all!

BIN WEEVILS ROCK

Clott

Tink

HAPPY HALLOWEEN!

FRAMED CELEBRITY PICS

COOL POSTERS

LED DISPLAY

CELEBRITY WALL STICKERS

CHALKBOARD

FISH WALL PLAQUE

SWS POSTERS

BIN WEEVIL

W.E.B
WEEVIL EXTERMINATION BUREAU

SECRET
WEEVIL SERVICE
sW2

SECRET
EVIL SERVICE
sW2

LIGHT UP YOUR LIFE

Light up your life with these amazing lamps, lanterns and spotlights!
Everything looks better with a little ILLUMINATION!

FISHBOWL LIGHT

TOP TIP
Place a row of lights along a back wall if you're displaying something really cool there, like a trophy shelf or collection. The lights will capture everyone's attention!

FAIRY FLOWER LIGHT

SKULL LANTERN

GLOWING VINE LIGHT

LOLLY FLOOR LAMP

And if you like to relax by firelight . . .

ROUND FIREPLACE

WITCH'S FIREPLACE

XMAS FIREPLACE

BRICK FIREPLACE

WEEVILY FIREPLACE

STONE FIREPLACE

TOP TIP

Pop an ornament on top of your fireplace – your mantelpiece doubles as a shelf. It's also a great place to leave milk and cookies for Santa!

ARE YOU A FAN?

Want a sweet poster of me to put up in your nest?

Of course you do! That's why I've got this fabulous gift for you – a signed Nest Inspector poster! Goodness me, I do hope that's my best angle.

The Nest Inspector

Solve the puzzle on the next page to complete a secret code that will unlock this marvellous poster!

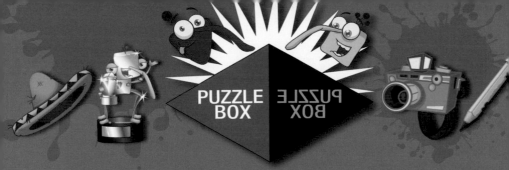

Each of these symbols represents a different number: **2, 4, 6** and **8**. Can you help me match each number to the correct symbol and solve the problems?

PROBLEM 1:

PROBLEM 2:

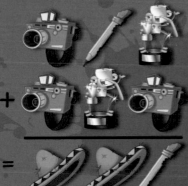

SECRET CODE: __ __ __ NEST __ __ __

MYSTERY CODE MACHINE

CLAIM YOUR PRIZE!

1. Fill in your solutions to both problems to complete the secret code (a number on each end!)
2. Visit the Mystery Code Machine outside Lab's Lab to redeem your code!

WHAT'S YOUR NEST DÉCOR STYLE?

Which famous Bin Weevil are you most like when it comes to nest decorating?

Complete this pop quiz to find out!

What's your favourite colour scheme?
A. Bold and bright primary colours.
B. Soft pastel shades or rainbow patterns.
C. Elegant gold, silver, black and white or grey.

You're looking for the perfect lighting to finish off your room. What do you pick?
A. An ultra-cool set of lanterns.
B. Cute flower fairy lights.
C. A gold chandelier.

What's underfoot in your favourite room?
A. Circus Floor – quirky and colourful.
B. Bunty Rug – sweet celeb style.
C. Dosh's Palace Rug – pure luxury.

40

When you go to the Haggle Hut, what's your tactic?

A. Throw a random assortment of items on to the counter, then Take A Chance!
B. Choose carefully which items you're willing to part with.
C. Keep passing items over to Nab until you've earned enough for that one top item you're saving up for!

Which trophies do you like best?

A. The weirdest and most nonsensical ones!
B. The ones that look like tasty treats!
C. The biggest, shiniest, most glittery ones!

MOSTLY As

ZING

RAZY COLLECTOR

Ve bet every inch of our nest is crammed with cool gadgets, zany ollectibles and nultitudes of patterns. doesn't matter if it natches – if you can nd a space for it, you'll isplay it proudly!

MOSTLY Bs

BUNTY

DAINTY DECORATOR

You design each room with utmost care and you like all your stuff to match. You can take ages designing a single room, but when you're done, we bet you invite every single buddy to take a look!

MOSTLY Cs

DOSH

LIVING IN LUXURY

The more expensive the item, the better! Your nest is dripping with gold, silver and bling of all kinds. Your buddies had better put their shades on when they drop in!

MIRROR MAZES

Dosh and Tink have each bought a new mirror to put up in their nest, but they've managed to misplace them already! Can you help each Bin Weevil find their mirror? (Answers on page 96!)

 START

42

START

PSSST! Hold this page up to a mirror to reveal a secret code below! You can redeem this code in the Mystery Code Machine in front of Lab's Lab to earn a cool prize!

BUG23REDE

43

PALACE LUXURY

We can't all live in a ruby-encrusted palace like Dosh, but with these glittering nest items, you'll feel like you do! These luxury buys may cost you little more, but they'll be well worth it when you're living it up like royalty!

MULCH THEME

MULCH NOTE WALLPAPER

PALACE THEME

DOSH'S PALACE FLOOR

ROYAL THRONES

DOSH'S PALACE CHAIR

MULCH LIGHT

PILE OF BLING

DOSH'S PALACE WINDOW

DOSH'S PALACE SHELF

TOP TIP
Guarantee a Royal Flush every time by purchasing the Golden Toilet from Grunt!

45

CELEBRITY STYLE

These super-stylish items made their debut at the Bin Weevils Celebrity Party and became instant hits! Every day is a party with your favourite stars when you've got these super sets in your nest.

CLOTT ROOM

CLOTT FIGURINE

CLOTT PILLOW SEAT

TOP HAT LAMP

TINK ROOM

TINK FIGURINE

TINK FLOOR LAMP

46

SCRIBBLES ROOM

TOP TIP
If you really want to feel like a star, add lots of impressive framed photos of yourself to the wall! To find out how, see pages 84–85.

MICROPHONE LAMP

SCRIBBLES TEDDY

BUNTY'S WALLPAPER

BUNTY ROOM

Oh my gosh, this is the best nest theme EVER!

BUNTY TEDDY

47

THINK TINK

For the green-fingered among you, there's a whole range of accessories to make you feel at one with nature. Tink's designed a whole set of nest items inspired by his famous Tree, and there's so much more! From potted plants to grass underfoot, don't be afraid to turn things inside out and bring the outside in.

POTTED TINK'S TREE

MUSHROO SHELF

BIN GARDEN SET

MUSHROO SEAT

This was a competition-winning design by **Binsy!**

There's no doub about it – an outdoorsy nest is t best kind of nest

CLASSIC VASE

TULIP VASE

DAISY VASE

SUNFLOWER VASE

POTTED DANCING DAISIES

POTTED SCENT FLOWERS

TOP TIP
Put a shelf on the front wall of your nest room to get the best view of your flowers or trophies!

49

FAIRYTALE FANTASY

Those fairytale characters always seem to have more fun, don't they! If you're never short of adventure or imagination and you're always off in your own magical world, then these theatrical props are an absolute must!

HEART SOFA

GIANT TEDDY

GOLD CARRIAGE

HEART THRONE

50

SWEET AS CANDY

Your nest will look good enough to eat with these sweet accessories! I recommend mixing and matching for a pick-and-mix variety room. Yum yum!

CUPCAKE ROOM SET

LITTLE SWEETS ROOM SET

RAINBOW SWEETS ROOM SET

CANDYFLOSS MACHINE

ICE CREAM TABLE

LOLLYPOP STOOLS

ICE CREAM STOOLS

BONBON CLOCK

LOLLY SWIRL RUG

STRAWBERRY CAKE BED

TOP TIP
Cupcake collectibles and yummy-looking trophies make great accessories for this theme!

BISCUIT SOFA

CUPCAKE COLLECTIBLES

ROCK CAFE WALLPAPER

TOP TIP
If you're having lots of guests over, make sure you have plenty of chairs for them to sit on!

ROCK CAFE FLOOR

SPEAKER WALLPAPER

HOT

RETRO CAR SOFA

DANCE FLOOR

CLUB FLING WALLPAPER

WEEVILY JUKEBOX

CLUB FLING DANCE FLOOR

FLING'S DANCE COSTUME

Winners of Fling's Dance-Off at the Celebrity Party earned this cool replica of Fling's prize-winning dance costume!

55

SPORTS FAN

If, like Gong, you're obsessed with all things sporty, then this is definitely the theme for you! Whether you love to zoom around the race track or showcase your talents on the football pitch, why not create a room that shows off your interests?

FOOTBALLS

FOOTBALL GOAL

BIN WEEVILS FLAGS

FOOTBALL BED

FOOTBALL PITCH FLOOR

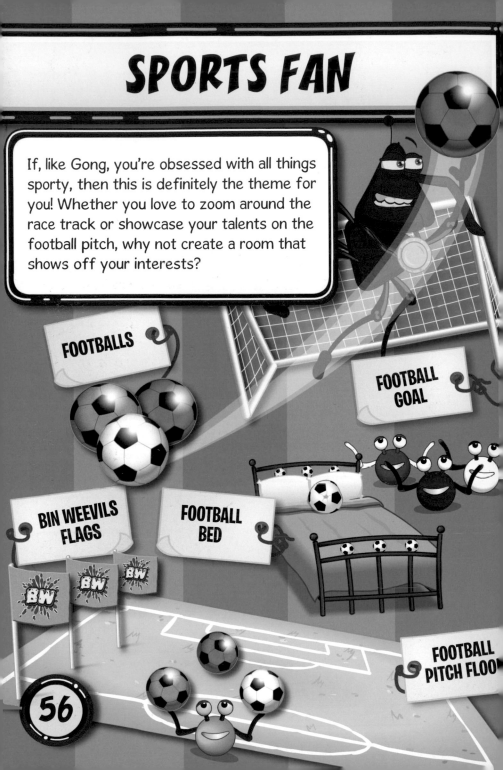

RACE CAR BEDS

W3Y1L 2

W3Y1L 3

WEEVIL WHEELS WALLPAPER

TOP TIP
Weevil Wheels trophies and the Level 25 boxing glove trophy would be awesome additions to any sports-themed room!

WEEVIL WHEELS FLOOR

SURFBOARD

BEACH BALL

HAM'S RACING FIGURINE

57

BIN CIRCUS

TRAPEZE TINK

Transform your nest into a big-top extravaganza with these show-stopping items!

BLUE CIRCUS TENT WALL

Check out these super-cool star circus floors!

RED CIRCUS TENT WALL

BUNCH OF BALLOONS

TIGHTROPE CLOTT

YELLOW CIRCUS TENT WALL

The Bin Circus theme was the winner of the very first Biggest Bin Wish competition. The grand prize winner, **chelsea 101**, came up with these daredevil designs!

CIRCUS CHAIR

TOP TIP
Teach your Bin Pet new tricks in a circus-themed room for extra fun!

CIRCUS DIVE POOL

CIRCUS BALL

STEPS DECORATION

ELEPHANT TRUNK

CIRCUS CANNON

UNDER THE SEA

Want to live under the sea? Cause a splash and transform your nest into a lovely bubbly underwater paradise with these sea-themed nest items!

OCTOPUS WALLPAPER

WHALE WALLPAPER

WAVES WALLPAPER

BUBBLY FISH WALLPAPER

WEEVILY MERMAID STATUE

TOP TIP
Mushroom seats and shelves can double as coral reefs!

CORAL BED

SHELL MIRROR

MAGIC SHELL COLLECTIBLES

TOP TIP
The Magic Shell collectibles make perfect accessories for this theme!

WHALE SOFA

MESSAGE IN A BOTTLE

UNDERWATER WINDOW

ℹ️ When you invite a friend to join Bin Weevils, you'll earn a giant wall aquarium for your nest! Every time you invite another friend, you'll be rewarded with a fish or critter for your aquarium. Try setting up your aquarium alongside your sea-themed items!

SUPER SAFARI

There's nothing like a day in the sun! Indulge your love of the wild and take your Bin Buddies on a super safari when they step through your door. Watch out for lions!

WOODEN ELEPHANT

SNAKE CHAIR

TRIBAL MASKS

TOP TIP
Collect all the Tribal Masks to complete your colourful room!

62

CHECKERED PILLOW SEAT

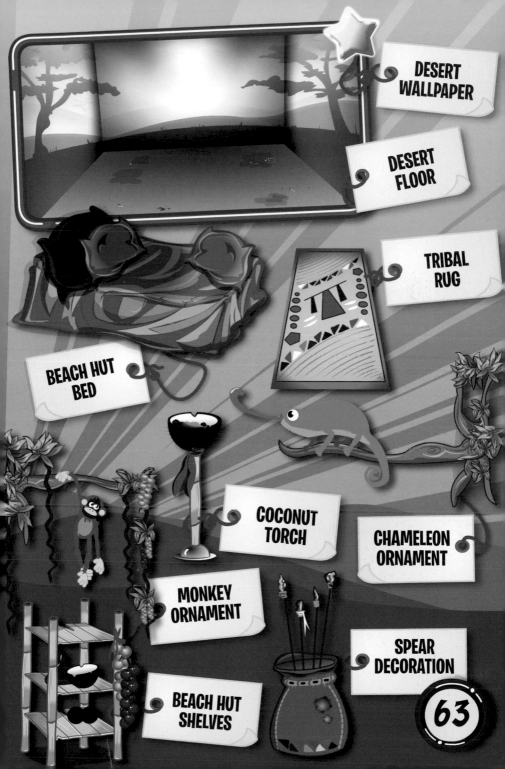

DESERT WALLPAPER

DESERT FLOOR

TRIBAL RUG

BEACH HUT BED

COCONUT TORCH

CHAMELEON ORNAMENT

MONKEY ORNAMENT

SPEAR DECORATION

BEACH HUT SHELVES

63

SPACED OUT

This theme is perfect for any budding astronauts, UFO spotters or alien enthusiasts! Wouldn't you love to gaze up at the planets from the comfort of your spaceship bed?

ROCKET SHIP BED

UFO BED

EGG CHAIR

TOP TIP

These egg-shaped chairs add a touch of space-age luxury to any nest – and they're comfy, too!

BW

SPACE ROCKET

OUTER SPACE WALLPAPER

NIGHT SKY RUG

LAVA LAMPS

INFLATABLE ALIEN

STAR & MOON LIGHTS

TOP TIP

Star light, star bright! Hang up some Star Lights to make your room feel like the centre of the galaxy!

65

ENCHANTED FOREST

Get swept away to a moonlit fairyland where magic is most certainly real. Who wouldn't want to relax beside this amazing enchanted pond, complete with lilypads!

MAGIC FIELD ROOM SET

WILLOW POND ROOM SET

FAIRY BED

SECRET TREE

FAIRY FLOWER LIGHT

TOADSTOOLS

HANGING LEAF SEAT

FUNKY FLOWER

GLOWING VINE LIGHT

BOWL OF APPLES

WOODEN SHELF

TOP TIP
Wooden tables, chairs and shelves make a great finishing touch for this theme!

LOG STOOLS & TABLE

67

LOOPY LABORATORY

Inspired by the Bin's biggest brainiac, this set is packed with everything you need to create your very own mad science lab. I'm not so sure about Lab's experiments, though – I wouldn't try those at home!

LAB'S WORKSHOP WALL

LAB'S LAB CEILING

LAB'S LAB FLOOR

TICKER TAPE MACHINE

HANGING BOOKSHELF

LAB'S
WORKSTATIONS

LAB'S POTION
JARS

TOP TIP
There are lots of
Potion Jars to collect.
No mad science lab is
complete without a
good selection of
potions!

MINIATURE
LAB'S LAB

HOLIDAY SPIRIT

CHRISTMAS

Bin Weevils just love getting into the holiday spirit at those special times of year . . . well, except for Bing, who's in the holiday spirit ALL the time. Check out these holiday-themed rooms for some fresh inspiration!

YULETIDE ROOM SET

STOCKING

PILE OF PRESENTS

XMAS FIREPLAC

PRESENT MAKER

I see no reason why you can't keep your holiday decorations out all year long. Who isn't up for a bit of festive cheer in July?

HALLOWEEN

BOO! Spookify your nest for Halloween with an assortment of slimy, creepy and crawly nest items!

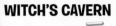
WITCH'S CAVERN

HALLOWEEN WALLPAPER

HANGING BAT

WEEVILY ZOMBIES

HANGING SPIDER

BUNNY CHAIR

HAPPY EASTER SIGN

EASTER

Hop to the shops to deck out your nest with all the signs of spring!

HALF EGG STOOL

71

MEDIWEEVIL TIMES

Wouldn't you love to journey back in time to become one of brave King Arthur's knights? The next best thing is this magical medieval nest item set, inspired by Castle Gam!

CASTLE GAM ROOM SET

TOP TIP
Pair some medieval accessories with the Gam's Dragon Wall to recreate Castle Gam's famous dungeons!

MEDIEVAL ROOM SET

72

HALBERD ORNAMENTS

REGAL ROOM SET

STAINED GLASS WINDOW

WEEVILY FOUNTAIN

MEDIEVAL HALL

WOODEN TABLE & BENCHES

A B C D
E F G H
I J K L
M N O
P Q R
S T U
V W X
Y Z

MEDIEVAL BANNER

Gam is so old that the history of the Bin is split into BG (Before Gam) and AG (After Gam). Nobody is quite sure how old he is, so nearly all Bin history is AG!

KNIGHT STATUES

73

PICK YOUR BUDGET

BIN BARGAIN

You don't need to spend a ton to whip up a super-stylish nest design! You can get your room off to a great start on a budget!

CASTLE GAM STYLE

Check out this mix of cool but inexpensive items!

WOODLAND THEME

FUN & GAMES THEME

Things don't always have to match to look great!

PLASMA BALL

BIN WEEVIL FIREPLACE

FLOWER MIRROR

CLOTT STICKER

SLIME TABLE

CUCKOO CLOCK

ROCKING HORSE

ROBOT HAND

BRICK FIREPLACE

BUBBLE MACHINE

INFLATABLE PARROT

FUNKY FLOWER

Got some items you don't really need any more? Take them to the Haggle Hut to trade them in for some extra Mulch!

WEEVIL WHEELS SHELF

75

PICK YOUR BUDGET

DELUXE DÉCOR

You've been busy saving up and now you're ready to give your nest a sweet upgrade! Here are some awesome items to add to your shopping list.

MOONLIT BALCONY

Check out this icy cool room! It's simply brrrr-illiant!

ICE CAVE ROOM

LAKE VIEW ROOM

Look at this gorgeous view! It's deluxe, darling!

CONFETTI CANNON

PILLOW SEAT

ANIMATED PICTURE

HOLLYWOOD VANITY

SECRET PICTURE FRAME

MULCH RECYCLING MACHINE

STONE FIREPLACE

PEEL PARK STATUE

MOSAIC CHAIR

MOSAIC TABLE

16TH CENTURY DRAWERS

TINK STONE SCULPTURE

The Mosaic Table and Chairs were a competition-winning design by HANNAHMONTANA1!

BONBON CLOCK

77

PICK YOUR BUDGET

SUPER-DELUXE SPENDER

Have you got a winning MULCH-TASTIC ticket?
Have you been saving up like crazy? The
sky's the limit and you're ready to go all-out
to make your nest a palace paradise!

You can now get your very own
humongous safe that fills the
entire back wall of your nest!

MEGA WALL SAFE

TYCOON ISLAND ROOM

DOSH'S PALACE COLLECTION

Collect all the Dosh's
Palace items and live
just like Dosh does!

PILE OF BLING

GOLDEN TOILET

GOLDEN FLING STATUE

HAM'S GOLDEN GUITAR

ELECTRIC GUITAR

DRUM KIT

DOSH'S PALACE CHAIR

WEEVILY JUKEBOX

X-RAY MACHINE

The more you spend, the more XP you earn, which will help you level up super-fast!

GOLD DISCO BALL

79

COLOUR PLAY

You don't have to theme every single room in your nest. Sometimes a clever colour combination is all you need to create the WOW factor!

MONOCHROME MAGIC
A uniform look can really make a nest stand out from the crowd!

PRETTY IN PINK

SINGIN' THE BLUES

PURPLE REIGN!

TOP TIP
Finish off your room by displaying some matching trophies or flower vases!

COORDINATE YOUR TROPHIES

BLACK 'N' WHITE
A super-sophisticated colour scheme that oozes elegance.

ROUND STAR RUG

LUXE SOFA

ECLECTIC
Love a bit of everything? Let loose with a rainbow of colour!

LOLLYPOP STOOL

81

TROPHIES

Ooooh, shiny! Who doesn't love trophies? From funky to slimy to glittery to golden, I love a roomful of these beauties. Here are some cool ways to display your achievements!

Trophies can be displayed on almost anything that has a surface – not just a shelf!

TOP TIP

The Level 12 eyeball trophy is perfect for a creepy-looking Halloween room!

82

LEVEL 3

LEVEL 6

LEVEL 11

LEVEL 4

LEVEL 18

LEVEL 33

LEVEL 27

LEVEL 40

LEVEL 28

LEVEL 52

LEVEL 43

LEVEL 61

LEVEL 64

LEVEL 53

LEVEL 23

LEVEL 30

TOP TIP
Garden-themed
trophies look
lush grouped
together!

83

SNAP-HAPPY

Make your nest really feel like home with some fun photos of you and your Bin Buddies!

Rockin' Rainbow!

Terrific Tree!

WEEVIL WEEKLY!

84

Awesome Office!

TOP TIP
Smaller frames cost less, and you can fit more than one on a wall!

Head over to a Tycoon Plaza to snap some pics, then select your favourite frames to show them off!

TOP TIP
Add some flair to your photos and tie your photo wall together with some bows!

You can see which plazas are open for business by clicking on the top hat outside the Shopping Mall. An open photo studio is marked with a camera icon.

SPECIAL NEST ITEMS

Bin Weevils can earn special nest items by completing SWS missions and entering competitions! I just love to see these prizes proudly displayed in a nest – they make me wonder about the weevily adventures these Bin Weevils have been on!

TOP TIP
Sign up to the Secret Weevil Service to complete exciting new missions!

SWS MISSION TROPHIES

WHAT'S NEW

TOP TIP

Keep an eye on the What's New Blog for the Weekend Puzzle Challenge — you could score an exclusive nest item and other rewards!

PUZZLE BOX

PUZZLE BOX

MINIATURE LAB'S LAB

BINFTA TROPHY

Here are just a few of the amazing prizes I've seen.

Celebrity Bowling!

BOWLING TROPHIES

CELEB CRIBS

Some of the Bin's most popular celebrities allowed me to photograph their nests this year, and I was completely blown away by their interior design skills! Can you guess which room belongs to which celebrity? (Answers on page 96!)

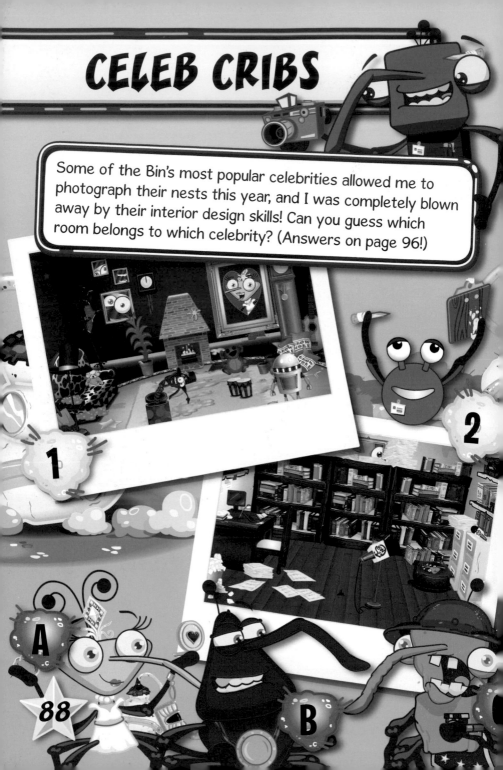

1

2

A

B

4

5

6

3

D

E

F

SPOT THE DIFFERENCE

90

Picture 1

I took two pictures of this BIN-tastic room, but I have a feeling that something has changed! Can you find ten differences between these pictures?

Picture 2

(Answers on page 96!)

MUDDLED MESSAGE

Uh-oh! I seem to have mixed up some of my words!

Unscramble the letters below to reveal seven words. (I said each of these words while visiting nests last week.) Then put all the shaded letters together to find out what word I exclaimed when I awarded a gold trophy! (Answers on page 96!)

ROTISPHE

DETCREOA

OUORLC

ULUFSABO

CLENIGI

ECORTSPIN

GNTIGILH

92   I EXCLAIMED: _ _ _ _ _ _ _ _ !

PENCIL PUZZLER

Oh dear! I've lost my pencil again!

Grrr, that's always happening to me while I'm busy admiring all those gorgeous nests!

I've lost eight PURPLE pencils like this one among the pages of this book. Can you find them all? Make a note of the page number where you find each pencil (in sequential order) to form a special code!

*Don't count the one I'm holding, I haven't lost it yet!

SECRET CODE:

— — — — — — — — — —

Good work, eagle eyes! Redeem your code at the Mystery Code Machine in front of Lab's Lab for a special surprise!

93

DID YOU KNOW?

JUNGLE MASKS

These masks belong to an ancient Bin tribe. Rumour has it that this tribe is responsible for building the Bin Pet temple on Mulch Island! To check out the temple for yourself, accept the 'Raiders of the Lost Bin Pet' mission with the SWS.

SWEET TROPHIES

Figg has a sweet tooth, and she's always baking delicious treats . . . but did you know that Figg is also an amazing sculptor? Check out these sweet trophies she's made!

INK'S ORANGE PEEL

Where did Ink's Orange Peel go? Nowhere! Clott accidentally shrank it with one of Lab's crazy inventions. That'll teach Lab to let Clott play with his high-tech toys!

PIANO

You can play and record your own weevily tunes on the piano! If you're a talented musician, don't forget to invite your buddies round for a listen!

GOODBYE

Oh! That's it? Have we finished already?
I could talk about nests all day!

Well, there you have it. You have all the information you need to get your weevily hands on one of my fabulous trophies!

Thanks for reading, and I hope you're well on your way to creating the BIN-tastic nest of your dreams. If you follow all my tips, you might have a Bin Nest trophy on your mantelpiece soon . . . Oooh la la!

See you around!

ANSWERS

PAGE 42-43 (MIRROR MAZES):

PAGE 88-89 (CELEB CRIBS):

A-3
B-6

PAGE 90-91 (SPOT THE DIFFERENCE):

No wallpaper

PAGE 92 (MUDDLED MESSAGE):

1. TROPHIES   5. CEILING
2. DECORATE   6. INSPECTED
3. COLOUR   7. LIGHTING
4. FABULOUS   8. EXCLAIMED